A FAR CRY FROM GANGLOTA

"Yassah's Cave"

TIKA SMITH

Life Chronicles Publishing
Give your life a voice!

ISBN: 978-1-950649-53-2
Editor: Julie Strong
Cover Design: German Creative

Life Chronicles Publishing Copyright © 2021

lifechroniclespublishing.com

This one's for you Daddy,
Tika

Foreword

A Far Cry From Ganglota is a real-life family story that reads like fiction. Tika Smith's first manuscript (part one) begins with Sam's story — he's a strapping young man with a bright future who had a way with the ladies — which proved to be complicated, messy, and quite lovely at the most critical times. His story begins in Monrovia, Liberia, on the West Coast of Africa in high school and unfolds with a series of events that would eventually take him and several of his family members to the United States. Smith shares Sam's love stories and heartbreaks, and his successes and regrets, and his emotional immigration story. It is raw, honest, and comes together like dominoes that eventually fall in a perfect line like they should. Sam's life was full of chain reactions that are still being felt by his children, and their children today. Smith used the 2020 pandemic to make sure her family history and the stories continue on by creating this first manuscript. When a person shares a true story about their family, it is always a special gift.

Lisa Patterson, Editor in Chief - 425 Magazine

TABLE OF CONTENTS

1. Sam 1

2. The Letters 5

3. Changes 9

4. Abroad 13

5. Unexpected News 15

6. Betrayal.. 21

7. The Coup 25

8. The End of the Beginning.................................... 29

1
SAM

Sam stood 6'4", about 160 pounds of pure muscles. He was dark-skinned with brown eyes. He was eye candy, and he knew it too! In high school, he always dressed to impress the ladies. Sam was a ladies' man and a mama's boy.

During his senior year of high school, he decided to protect and serve his community and country at large. So, he joined the police academy upon graduation. His charm and charisma followed him through the academy. After graduating with honors, he joined the police force in Monrovia, Liberia and was quickly promoted to the head of special security of Liberia's former president, President William R. Tolbert.

Liberia is a country on the west coast of Africa. A country known to the rest of Africa as "Small America." Liberia began as a settlement of the American

Colonization Society. ACS believed that the freed black slaves would have a better life if returned to their land. The Society then secured the land and shipped the freed slaves between 1822 and the American Civil War. In 1847, Liberia was granted its independence, making it the first independent Democratic Republic in Africa. Monrovia, the capital, is named after the former president of the United States, James Monroe.

Although Sam loved his job very much, he didn't feel complete. So, he decided to take classes at the University of Liberia. His major was business, following in his dad's footsteps.

A couple of years after his promotion in the police force, Sam and five of his coworkers were traveling from a rural area of the country when another driver t-boned their police van; their van was totaled. Everyone was injured except for Sam; he was built tough. Sam checked on the other vehicle's driver and found him badly wounded and non-responsive. He then radioed in for help. As much as he could, he tried to keep everyone stable until the ambulance and police backup arrived.

When they arrived at the OPD (ER), Sam locked his eyes on one person in particular after reporting to the healthcare team. She was light-skinned, very petite with a smile from Heaven. Long, beautiful hair with the prettiest dimples and teeth. He could not get his eyes off her!

He finally realized that he was undressing her with his eyes, piercing through her very soul. He turned and walked towards the nurse's station where his uncle was standing. Ernest, Sam's uncle was a nurse at the Firestone Hospital's OPD. "Uncle Ernest! Who is that beauty?" He asked. "ah hahhh!" Ernest laughed. "I see you've snapped out of your daydreaming! Her name is Christine. Christine Mulbah is her name. Go and introduce yourself."

"I cannot! I'm too embarrassed. Besides, I'm on duty." Sam replied.

"Ohhhh, now you're on duty, huh? I'm glad you've realized that!" Ernest replied.

They both laughed, hugged each other, and Sam was back on his way to the city.

As the days passed, he couldn't stop thinking about Christine. So, he decided to write her a letter, introducing himself and expressing his feelings for her. He put a picture of himself in the envelope and gave it to John, a distant relative who lived with Sam in the city. Sam had also enrolled him into the police academy, and upon completion, got him a job at the police station. "John, I need you to drive to Firestone and deliver this letter to a nurse by the name of Christine. Make sure she gets it!" "Right away, sir," John replied. Firestone was about an hour's drive from the state's capital, Monrovia.

2
THE LETTERS

The letters kept going back and forth between Sam and Christine. After a month of being pen pals, Sam drove to Firestone to meet Christine. They hit it off instantly. After a few months of dating, the handsome bachelor hung up his players' jersey for the woman of his dreams. They were inseparable. Sam would take Christine out to eat on several occasions before making a decision to meet his mom.

Finally, he took her to meet his mom, Yassah, to gain her approval. Christine had an angelic smile that would steal anyone's heart, even Sam's mom. Yassah was very picky about whom her son dated. The only thing Sam's mother shunned was the fact that Christine had a child from a previous relationship. But her golden boy was no saint. He had three kids (two girls and a boy) from previous relationships.

However, Christine checked all of the boxes that would require her blessing for her to date her son. She was a beauty with brains. While Christine waited in the living room, Yassah called Sam into her room. She told Sam that she gave them her blessing to be married.

After six months of dating, Sam decided it was time to pop the question. In the company of loved ones, he asked Christine to marry him, and she accepted his hand in marriage. They had a beautiful wedding ceremony six months after their engagement.

Because they both worked two hours apart, Christine remained in her apartment in Firestone, close to work, and Sam stayed in Monrovia. He would drive down on the weekends to be with his newly married wife.

A few months after their wedding, Christine found out that she was pregnant. They were very excited! He wanted to have a baby with his beautiful wife. From the moment he laid eyes on her, he knew then that she would be the mother of his children to come.

Sam asked a very close friend, who happened to be the department's director, to be the Godparent for their son. E. Richard Jones was their son's name, after his

Godfather. A year after their son Richard was born, they moved to Monrovia to live with her husband. She found a job at the John F Kennedy medical hospital.

Sam decided he wanted to go into business. He purchased a farm in Lofa County, where his mother was born. A rubber farm in a town called Ganglota. That farm was his pride and joy. He enjoyed spending vacations there with his wife, mother, and kids. The farm also generated a nice amount of income for him. This made him discover that he had a passion for the business world.

Little did Sam know, God was preparing his future for retirement from the public sector, a thought he never entertained. He loved his career as a police officer so much, he would remain until he couldn't work anymore. His business was a side hustle.

3
CHANGES

Christine applied for a nurse internship program abroad and got accepted into the program. This meant that it would take a year of clinical training in New York at First Presbyterian Hospital. Thoughts ran through her head about all of the skills she would learn to bring back to her peers in Liberia. Excited and anxious to share the great news with her king, she surprised him at work. She walked into his office, and as she opened the door, a young lady who was sitting on his desk quickly hopped off.

"Oh, hi dear! Christine said.

What a huge surprise!" Sam exclaimed.

"I'm sorry, did I interrupt something?!" Christine said in her calm, angelic voice.

"Oh, don't be silly!" Sam replied.

"Sabah, meet my wife, Christine."

Turning to Christine, he said, "This is Sabah. She's a cousin of mine. I recently hired her as my secretary. She came into the office to take notes for me. I'll be heading into a meeting shortly."

"Oh, very nice to meet you, Sabah. Who are your parents?!" Turning back to her husband, Christine asked, "Have I met them?"

"No, you haven't. They don't live near." Sam replied.

Sabah smiled and said to Christine, "It's nice meeting you too. I'll leave you both.

"Honey is everything okay at home?!" He asked.

"Everything is just fine, dear! I come bearing good news that I couldn't hold in! "You're pregnant?" Same screamed! "No dear, I got accepted into the nursing study program abroad!" Christine replied.

"Oh, honey, that's such great news! I'm so happy and proud of you! Let's celebrate when I get home this evening!" He gave her a big hug and a kiss, then walked her downstairs to get into her car.

The Simpsons enjoyed a beautiful evening celebrating Christine's acceptance to study abroad. Her departure was set for August 28th, just two months away. They had to think about who would stay with their four kids while Christine was away for a year! Her son from a previous relationship would go to live with his dad while she was away. Christine had a younger sister that she could ask to stay with the kids, but her husband quickly said, "No, dear. Sabah can stay with the kids. It'll be perfect."

"But didn't she just get a job at the station? I don't want to impose." Christine said.

"It's no big deal! She's my secretary, so she can work from here while watching the kids." Sam replied.

There was no convincing Sam otherwise! His idea was perfect, and it was either that or no study abroad for Christine.

"Okay, Sam, if you're sure she's going to be okay with it! However, I don't want to impose." Christine said.

"She will be fine; just leave it to me." Sam replied.

4
ABROAD

Christine left her kids to study abroad. At the airport, she had mixed emotions about leaving the love of her life and two sons she cherished so deeply. It was the hardest decision of her entire life, but she knew this move would be life-changing for her family. She was embarking upon the greatest opportunity of a lifetime! The kids, all five of them, accompanied Sam and Christine to the airport.

Tears and hugs were shared by all as she boarded the Pan American for The Big Apple! With a teary eye, Christine hugged Sam and told him to please take good care of the kids. She hugged her babies tight and told them to behave and that she would bring them all the latest gifts from abroad.

"I promise we'll be real good and not get into any trouble. HMMMA! I promise," said baby Richard, as he sobbed.

Christine called home every evening to check on her husband and kids. She worried about her kids. Not that anyone would harm them, just because she was such a caring mom, and this was her very first time being so far away from her kids this long.

Her boys were her whole existence! If she could, she would have taken them with her.

Christine knew her sacrifice was for the betterment of her family, so as much as she missed being with them, she studied twice as hard to get her internship done with flying colors. Her husband and kids depended on it. Her country depended on it.

5
UNEXPECTED NEWS

A year after the program was the following June. Christine completed her training with perfect grades and a letter of recommendation from the hospital's Chief of Staff. She then headed back to Liberia to be with her family! Fifteen hours of flying, and she could hold her babies in her arms again!

They all went to the airport to meet her, just like every time she traveled. But this time, it was different. This was the longest she'd ever been away from home.

"Cousin Sabah, thanks so much for taking care of the children," Christine said. "Anytime," Sabah replied. Christine gave Sabah a beautiful outfit that she bought from the states as a token of appreciation.

"OMG, I LOVE IT! Thanks so much! Sabah replied.

"Let's get your belongings into the car so the driver can give you a lift home," Sam told Sabah. Sabah said her goodbyes and was on her way. The kids had grown to love her.

It was a second honeymoon for the Simpsons! Three months after her return to Liberia, Christine found out that she was pregnant! Sam was elated to hear the good news! "Lord, please give me a girl, and this will be my very last child," she prayed out loud." "Yes, Lord! OUR last baby," Sam also prayed out loud as he kissed his wife on the forehead and hugged her tightly.

The honeymoon didn't last long. Sam started pulling late hours at the police station, and Christine saw less and less of him. When she was about six months pregnant, two of her cousins came to her with some news-You know what they say, "you don't have to pay for gossip." Her cousins told her that they heard that Sam and Sabah were not cousins, and as a matter of fact, they were dating. Also, he'd rented an apartment for Sabah not too far from the police station, and that's where he was spending most of his time. Christine shut down the rumors. "Nonsense," she said. "That lil girl is very respectful, and she took good care of the kids while I was abroad! She is Sam's cousin and nothing else!" "How can people spread such lies? How could he possibly date his own cousin?" Her cousins apologized and left Christine believing what she wanted to believe. After all, they didn't have any proof. It was all rumors.

Christine was now eight months pregnant, and the rumors resurfaced about her husband cheating with his so-called cousin. This time her cousins came with receipts. They knew exactly where Sabah lived, and Sam's car was over there lots of times! Even at times when he was supposedly working. Not only did they come to set the record straight about the relationship, but they also told Christine that Sabah was pregnant by Sam! Christine was speechless! She'd already confronted Sam months previously about the dating rumors to which he laughed at how absurd they sounded. "How could this be possible," she thought. "If you don't believe us, have your driver take us to her place and ask her who she's pregnant by." her cousin Elizabeth suggested. Christine was going to put the rumors to rest! She was so close to her due date and just wanted peace. "Okay, let's go; I'll ask her and put both of you to shame with your nonsense!"

As they approached the compound, they saw Sabah sitting on her porch. Christine got out of the car, and her cousins followed behind her.

"Hey, cousin Sabah! I haven't seen you in so long; how have you been?" She asked.

"Hello, Christine. I'm doing well." Sabah replied.
Sabah was indeed pregnant.

"Oh wow! You're also pregnant! Who are you pregnant by, and how far along are you?" Christine asked.

"I'm just two months pregnant. I'm pregnant by some boy. You don't know him. He's not from around here." Sabah replied.

"Oh, okay then. Congrats to you both. I just came to check up on you." Christine said.

"Okay, thanks for checking, Christine. Safe drive home. My love to the children." Replied Sabah.
Christine said goodbye and walked towards the car with her cousins. Her cousins didn't believe anything Sabah said, but Christine did, and that's all that mattered. Her

driver dropped them both off at their homes and then took Christine back home. As soon as she entered the yard, Sam was waiting for her at the door. He was very angry!

"Why would you embarrass Sabah like that?" What do you mean? Christine replied.

"You went to her house with your cousins to ask her who she was pregnant by?" "That's her personal business! None of yours! Don't you ever do that again!" Sam said.

Christine was so confused! Why would Sabah call Sam and tell him about her visit? What did she do wrong? "The rumors must be true then. All of it! That's why Sam was so mad!" she thought to herself. She went to the room, took a hot shower, and cried herself to sleep while Sam spent the night in the guest room.

6
BETRAYAL

A month later, on Valentine's Day, the Simpsons welcomed baby number two into the world! They both got their wish, a baby girl. Sam named her after his mother, Yassah, meaning the head of the village, and Christine gave her the name Aahlada, meaning my heart's desire. Aahlada looked everything like her daddy! Christine was in love all over again. Her baby girl and last baby. She had rough pregnancies and underwent caesareans for all three kids, so she was indeed done now that she had her heart's desire, a daughter.

A week later, after the birth of Aahlada, Sam made another visit to ELWA Hospital to take them home. His mother, Yassah, along with other family members, were at their home to welcome baby Aahlada. Grandma

Yassah stayed over four months to help Christine out around the house, and they also got a live-in nanny to take care of the other kids. (In Liberia, a nanny is called a house girl.) Dohmua was a girl from Ganglota who lived not too far from Yassah's Cave, the Rubber Farm. She sold produce at the community market, and Grandma Yassah told her parents that she wanted her in the city with her son and his wife. There she'd stay and help out around the house in exchange for an education. Because she was the oldest of her siblings, Dohmua's parents welcomed the idea. They knew their daughter would have a decent life in the city, gaining an education.

Christine had all the help that she needed and was recovering from her c-section very well. Baby Aahlada was now six months old, and Christine was ready to get back to work. Just a few weeks after returning to work, she got wind that Sabah was admitted to JFK hospital, where she worked to give birth to her baby. She also heard that her husband, Sam, was present at birth, and the baby looked just like him. Sabah gave birth to a baby girl. Sabah and the baby were discharged just days before Christine returned to work. Perfect timing on Sam's part. He made sure Christine didn't return to work until Sabah was discharged to go home. The gossip was all over the hospital. It was Sam's child, and he was present at her birthing.

Christine was heartbroken. How could the man she loved and the girl he introduced as his cousin betray her like that? She treated Sabah like family, and the whole time, she was pretending to be Sam's cousin. Their kids called her Aunty Sabah out of respect. There was nothing left to do. The answers were all there. The hurt and shame were too much to take, so she quietly started looking for a job in a county about four hours away from Monrovia.

When Aahlada turned a year old, Christine was hired as a nurse in the maternity ward at Bong Mines Hospital in Bong County. A fresh new start for her and her kids. She told Sam about her decision to move, and she moved with her two kids, Richard, then 8, and Aahlada 1. Their house girl Dohmua also moved with Christine and the kids. Sam would travel to Bong Mines every weekend to see her and the kids. It was almost like old times, where they both lived in separate households, except this time he was also with Sabah and their child. Because of their young kids, Christine decided not to get a divorce. She told herself that she would stick it out.

After trying to make things work for nine more years, Christine had come to the end of her rope. She couldn't hang in there anymore, so she filed for a divorce. After all of the begging and pleading by Sam to stay in the marriage to save face. Sam moved out of their house and into Sabah's apartment. Christine found out that Sam and Sabah had recently given birth to their second child together, another girl. There was no way she was going to forgive that. She'd had enough.

7
THE COUP

The Coup of 1980 changed Liberia. The economy was hurting, and the country wasn't safe anymore. Many of Christine and Sam's loved ones lost their lives during this time. Sabah and her girls were safe in the city and Sam was lucky to be alive. However, the government was looking for him, but he was able to escape to Bong Mines, where he hid for months until things calmed down. His uncle Ernest who once worked with Christine, also got hired as a nurse at the Bong Mines Hospital. Sam hid at his house for almost a year until things calmed down with the new government. Some of his colleagues were imprisoned, all because of the new government. Sabah and her girls were safe in the city.

Christine and her kids moved to the states a year later. Once there, she learned that Sam and Sabah had a marriage ceremony while away at her dad's feast. Her father had passed away, and so they planned a secret wedding during the feast with all of Sabah's family in attendance. Grandma Yassah was also in attendance. After the feast, they moved into Sam's house. The house that he and Christine built together to raise their kids in. The house that they thought they would grow old together in.

Sam was now a businessman full time. He wanted nothing to do with the government. It's amazing how God prepared him for such a time. His business was doing so well that it provided for his family, and he didn't have to work for a corrupt government. A government ruled by an indigenous man who killed a lot of Sam's close friends, relatives, and police chief.

Unfortunately, Sam's peace did not last long because the government sent troops to his house. They needed him back. A group of military officials showed up at Sam's house one night. The bang on the door woke up everyone. The house boy, asleep in his quarters, proceeded towards the entryway when he saw Sam at the top of the staircase. Sam signaled at him, giving him the go-ahead to see who was at the door. "Who is it?" said the house boy. "Open the door immediately! We are with the government, and we must speak with your boss!" Sam again signaled at the houseboy to open the door. As soon as the door was unlocked and open, the soldiers, about six of them, rushed over to Sam, put a rice bag over his head to blindfold him, handcuffed him, and threw him in the back of a van. His wife, kids, and house staff watched helplessly. The soldiers drove away with Sam without uttering a word to anyone.

They threw Sam into a cell and tortured him for hours. They beat him mercilessly while one of them set fire to the rice bag on his head. He suffered burns to his head and hair. This beating went on for hours before they left him on a dirty floor in a dark cell. He had no idea where he was because they kept him blindfolded. The night turned into day, and the day turned into night with Sam alone and helpless in a cell.

It was 11:59 the following night when a soldier entered the cell. He removed the burnt rice bag from Sam's head. "Mr. Simpson, Sir! You probably do not know me, but I know you very well. I cannot tell you

27

my name, but I've come to save you," the guard said. "They're going to torture you and then kill you. You're a good man, and you do not deserve any of this! You've helped my family, and so I will help you escape. Someone is waiting out this window for you, and they'll be taking you directly to the airport! Your wife and kids are already there waiting for you. You must leave the country tonight, or you will be dead by morning!" The guard then opened up the window and helped Sam out. He was immediately taken into the getaway car and headed to the airport, no questions asked. Sam was dropped off at the airport and helped into a private jet. Already on board the plane was his wife and their two daughters. They flew off into the night for the US.

8
THE END OF
THE BEGINNING

Upon arrival to the states, Sam was rushed to the ER to treat his severe burn to the head and bruises from the beatings that he endured while he was held captive. He and his family were then taken to a family member's home to stay until they got their own place.

Sam laid in his bed for days, thinking about the crazy chain of events that had taken place in his life over a span of 48 hours. He thought about the man who came into his cell and saved his life. *How well did the guard know him that he would put his life on the line to save his? What happened to that guard? Did they kill him after they discovered Sam was gone? Did they torture him?* Those were some of the questions that ran through his mind while recovering physically and mentally.

It didn't take Sam long to get back on his feet. Within a month he had regained his strength. He then applied for asylum, and it was granted. They finally moved into a place of their own.

Sam began to wonder about his first wife and children. He decided to take a trip to Massachusetts to reunite with his kids from Christine, his first wife. Sam was always in contact with his Christine and the kids. They had a solid bond that neither distance, time, nor circumstances could break. Especially his bond with Aalada.

About a year after their relocation to the United States, the Simpsons began looking for employment. Sam found a job as a security officer, and his wife got a job as a personal care assistant at a group home. It was quite the downgrade from their fabulous life in Liberia. While he worked as a security guard in the United States, he had to hire security to guard his home in Liberia. Here he was, in America working as a guard. Sam was so happy to have escaped death by torture in Liberia; his new life didn't bother him one bit! He was an excellent security officer, and his job was fortunate to have him.

But there was trouble in paradise at home. His wife started to become distant.

On a frigid winter night, Sam came home from work to a very cold and dark apartment. Sabah and the girls had left him. She emptied everything out of the apartment and turned off the electricity. Sam didn't see any of this coming. He thought they had been robbed, and his family was in danger. He immediately called Sabah, but she wouldn't answer any of his calls. He reached over to his work bag and got his flashlight to look for clues before calling the cops. There, on the kitchen counter, was a note from Sabah that read:

"Sam, the girls, and I are gone to live in Missouri with my cousin. Please do not come looking for us. Please do not call me. It's over between us." That was the only explanation he received.

Sam fell to his knees weeping! His whole world had come tumbling down. He laid on the carpet in his uniform until the next morning.

Sam got everyone he knew to beg Sabah to come back home. He even went as far as asking Christine to beg Sabah, the person he cheated on Christine with! Being the sweet and caring person, Christine saw how the breakup had taken a toll on Sam. She talked to Sabah and begged her to go back home, but Sabah wasn't hearing any of it. She had moved on, and there was no turning back for her.

A year after his separation from Sabah, Sam started to have fainting episodes at work. After his second episode of fainting, he was rushed to the ER by ambulance and admitted to the hospital. His nephew immediately called his daughter, Aahlada, who lived in Arizona. Christine, his first wife also lived in Arizona with her daughter. Aahlada took the first flight out to be by her dad's side. She loved her father so much, and she was his whole world.

Aahlada rushed to the hospital as soon as she landed to be by her dad's side. Sam was so happy to see her. While visiting with his daughter, Sam's attending physician also stopped by to see him.

"Can I please have a word alone with your father?" Dr. Smith asked.

"Oh, absolutely!" She replied. "I'll go check on mom and the kids, dad." She kissed her dad on the forehead and went into the family waiting room to call her mom and kids.

"You need to tell your daughter what is going on, Sam. You cannot go through this alone." Dr. Smith advised. Sam had to come clean to his baby girl. Aahlada was called back into the room, and Dr. Smith told her the bad news.

Sam had Stage Four Prostate Cancer. It was discovered late, and it metastasized to the bones. Aahlada looked at her dad and started crying. *Why him? Such a strong and loving father. How did this happen to him? But then was soon reminded of what a strong man her father was.* "We're gonna fight this, dad! You're going to be just fine!" "Yes, we will, baby girl! Yes, we will!" Aahlada leaned in and gave her dad a big old hug.

That was it. The secret was out. Aahlada called all of the family members, including Sabah and her girls, to inform them of her father's illness. Sam was discharged to go home a few days later, and Aahlada flew back to Arizona.

Sam flew to Arizona for the first time to spend Thanksgiving with Aahlada and her kids. They had the

33

best Thanksgiving ever. He apologized to Aahlada and Christine for all of the hurt and pain he caused them by ruining his marriage and family.

With the news of Sam's terminal illness, there was nothing to discuss. They hugged him and cried and decided that day to let go of the past hurt and pain he caused. Aalada made sure of that.

Upon Sam's return to Maryland after a week in Arizona, he started to get sick again. He was rushed to the hospital, and Aahlada flew down to be with him. This time he was in the ICU and put on a ventilator. He pulled through, and three days later, he was taken off the ventilator and breathing on his own. His doctor stopped by to talk to him. He informed him that they would need to amputate his left foot to save his life. Sam had diabetes and high blood pressure as well. The news of his leg being amputated hit him much harder than being diagnosed with prostate cancer. Sam was a very independent man and now finding out that he needed to depend on someone else for the rest of his life didn't sit well with him.

Aahlada knowing her dad, told Dr. Smith that her dad wouldn't stay in rehab, so she would move to take care of him. And so, it was settled!

On Dec 23rd, Aahlada decided to fly back to Arizona and spend Christmas with her kids. She was a single mother and never spent the holidays without them. She leaned in, hugged her dad goodbye and said, "I'll be back with the kids in two weeks, dad! You hang in there." As she walked out of the room, Sam's eyes followed her. He kept looking at her until she was no longer in sight.

Sam was doing so much better! On New Year's Day, his niece went to visit him, and she called Aahlada so that Sam could talk to her. "Happy New Year!" He said, struggling to get the words out. A huge improvement! Before Aahlada left him, he couldn't talk. Everyone communicated with him using a chalkboard. She was so happy to hear her daddy's voice. A very happy new year indeed! "Oh, daddy, you sound so good! I can't wait to see you; just one more week, and I'll be there!"

On January 7th, Aahlada got a phone call from Sam's nurse. It was a call she wasn't expecting. She was told that Sam had taken a change for the worse, and this time they didn't expect him to make it overnight. "Thanks for calling, Aahlada said to the nurse. We're driving down tomorrow. I know my dad will pull through just fine, just like he did before!"

The next day, Aahlada and her kids, mom, and older brother Richard started their road trip to Maryland. She had begged her mom to move to Maryland with her and help take care of her dad. Her brother, was riding along to go visit his dad for the first time since his illness. Just 45 minutes into the drove, she received a call from her cousin.

"Are you driving?" He asked.

"I am." Aahlada replied.

"Pull over to the side of the road so we can talk." Tom said.

Aahlada quickly pulled over to the side.

"The papay just died!" He said to Aahlada, crying. A loud scream from the depths of her belly poured out. The phone was on speaker. Her mom and brother heard the bad news and also began to cry. Aahlada's world stood still for about 10 minutes. "Dear God, why?" Why was the love of her life taken away from her? Why did she leave his bedside? Why didn't he fight just a little while longer? Why, why, why?

Aahlada got herself together and started to drive again. Her request to the hospital was to leave her daddy at the hospital until she got there to say her final goodbye. She did not want to do this in a funeral home; she wanted him right in that hospital bed where she left him.

While driving, Aahlada received a phone call from her uncle. Sam's estranged wife had instructed the hospital to have the body released to a funeral home. Sabah was called the night before Sam's death and immediately got on a plane with her kids to Maryland. She was still legally married to Sam. Although she wasn't in his life the whole time he was sick, she exercised her wifely powers to call all the shots as he took his last and final breath.

Aahlada was heartbroken. She arrived at the hospital and ran up to the floor her dad was on. She walked into the room and looked at the bed that he once occupied. Not a sign of him. Not even his sweet smell of eucalyptus mint oil that she'd massaged his body with. The linens had been stripped off the bed, the same way her daddy had been stripped out of her life. The nurse who placed the phone call to Aahlada walked into the room to console a devastated Aahlada. "I'm so very sorry for your loss," the nurse said as she hugged Aahlada. They hugged for about 5 minutes, as Aahlada sobbed helplessly.

As she walked past the room, she looked back at the bed and broke down into tears again. Those eyes that followed her until she was no longer in sight two weeks prior were no longer there. If only she knew that would have been her last time seeing him, they would've spent one last Christmas and New Year together. This would cause Aahlada feelings of guilt for years to come.

Sam was buried. His wife and her daughters planned the whole funeral without any input from his first family. Aahlada was devastated but had to keep quiet so that her dad would be buried in peace. She knew that's what he would have wanted.

A week after his burial, Sabah went over to pack up Sam's apartment with his nephew Tom. Aahlada received a phone call from Tom; he asked her if she wanted her dad's furniture and tons of his books. Her dad was an avid reader. "Of course." Aahlada replied! She would take anything to hold on to her dad's memories. When she arrived at the apartment to collect her dad's things, she noticed that they had ransacked his belongings looking for deeds and his will. However, they did not find a will.

Back home in Liberia, things were hard for Sam junior and his sister Karen. They no longer had their source of financial support. Karen placed a call to Aahlada asking for help. Sabah had traveled to Liberia and served Karen with a 30 day vacate notice from their Monrovia family home. This was the house that Sam and Christine built together. Sabah had gone back home to take over all of Sam's property, including the farm in Ganglota. Aahlada was furious after hearing such news. But there wasn't anything anyone could do. There was no will, and Sabah was his legal wife, so she had all rights to Sam's estate.

Aahlada had a space in her basement decorated in memory of her father, and she would go there daily to talk with her dad. Next to the shrine that she had decorated so beautifully was a bookcase with all of Sam's books. On this day, much like any other day, she went down to the basement to pray and talk to her dad. On her way back up the stairs to the living room, she accidentally hit the bookcase, and a few books fell off. One book in particular fell and opened, and a piece of paper fell out. Aahlada opened up the document, and there it was. Sam's will! She couldn't believe her eyes. In that will, Sam had left most of his estate to her. Sabah was nowhere in the will. Aahlada couldn't believe her eyes! She fell to her knees, crying and thanking God. The will literally fell into the right hands just as Sam had wanted.

Aahlada called her dad's lawyer right away! His lawyer told her that her dad rewrote his will with him when he was sick. He informed her to go to her bank and get it notarized! And so she did! She ran to her bank with Sam's identification cards that she had and the will. She then sent a copy to her sister in Liberia and a notarized letter giving Karen temporary possession of the house and her brother Sam Jr. temporary possession of the rubber farm and house in Ganglota.

Sabah had her day in court. Not only did the reading of Sam's will by the judge come as a total shock to her, but Sam and Christine were never legally divorced. Sam told Christine he would sign the divorce papers and file them himself. Christine left it to him and assumed it was done. She never asked him for copies of the divorce filing. It all made perfect sense now. No wonder why Sam and Sabah didn't have a big wedding.

They eloped, and only their kids were in attendance. None of Sam's other kids were invited to the wedding, and they were told about the nuptials after they were married.

On the farm, Sam junior took complete possession of all rubber sales income. He wouldn't even help his sister Karen out. Everyone pleaded with him, but he played deaf to their pleas. He was an alcoholic and also did drugs. He answered to no one.

One day, his dad appeared to Sam Jr in a daydream, telling him what he was doing was wrong, that he was an embarrassment to the family and his legacy! He told him to stop what he's doing. "Get away from me! Sam junior cried out," I can do what I want! You're not the boss of me! Go away from here!"

Sam junior fell to his knees and buried his sobbing face in the palm of his hands. When he removed them minutes later and opened his eyes, there was no one there. He didn't see nor hear his dead father anymore. He got up from his knees, walked toward the farmhouse, held his chest, and collapsed to the ground.

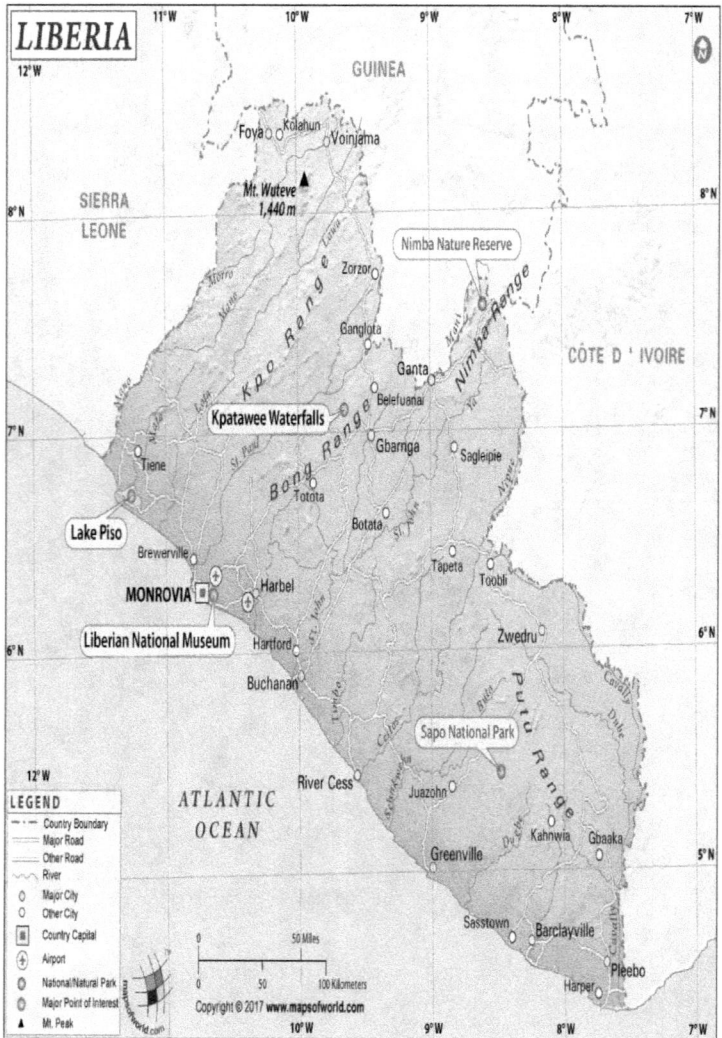

LIBERIA

11° W 10° W 9° W 8° W 7° W
12° W

GUINEA

Foya Kolahun Voinjama

Mt. Wuteve
1,440 m

8° N

SIERRA
LEONE

Zorzor

Nimba Nature Reserve

Ganglota

Ganta

K p o   R a n g e

Belefuanai

Kpatawee Waterfalls

CÔTE D ' IVOIRE

7° N

B o n g   R a n g e

N i m b a   R a n g e

Gbarnga Sagleipie

Tiene

Totota

Botata

Lake Piso

Brewerville

Tapeta Toobli

MONROVIA Harbel

Liberian National Museum Hartford

Zwedru

6° N

Buchanan

P u t u   R a n g e

Sapo National Park

12° W

River Cess Juazohn

ATLANTIC
OCEAN

Kahnwia Gbaaka

Greenville

5° N

Sasstown Barclayville

Pleebo

Harper

LEGEND
— · — Country Boundary
──── Major Road
──── Other Road
∿∿∿ River
○ Major City
○ Other City
▣ Country Capital
✈ Airport
○ National/Natural Park
○ Major Point of Interest
▲ Mt. Peak

0   50 Miles
0   50   100 Kilometers
Copyright © 2017 www.mapsofworld.com

10° W 9° W 8° W 7° W